Keep Calm
and
Trust God

VOLUME 2

BY
JAKE PROVANCE
&
KEITH PROVANCE

Keep Calm and Trust God — Volume 2
ISBN: 978-1-939570-53-6
Copyright © 2015 by Word and Spirit Publishing

Published by Word and Spirit Publishing
P.O. Box 701403
Tulsa, Oklahoma 74170

Creative concept by Ryan Provance

Table of Contents

Introduction

This is volume two of the "The Keep Calm & Trust God" series. Volume one received such a positive response that at the encouragement of our readers, we have decided to expand the series. We hope it will bless you and encourage you in your faith, so that even if trials and troubles seem unavoidable, you will be prepared to keep calm, and trust God.

During World War II, as the conflict intensified, Winston Churchill and the British government realized that an invasion of England was imminent. The government had thousands of posters printed with the slogan "Keep Calm & Carry On." In the event that Hitler's army invaded Britain, the posters were to be distributed to the British general population in an effort to galvanize their resolve to resist German aggression. If indeed

Germany did invade Britain, it would be one of the darkest hours in British history and the history of the free world. Many believed it would be the final opportunity to prevent Hitler's complete domination of Europe.

Under the shadow of Nazi air raids and bombing runs, death and destruction, and a world thrown into chaos, the British knew the people would need encouragement. The future of the free world teetered in the balance. And in those dark times, believers everywhere prayed fervently.

Thankfully, most of us will never have to face that kind of tragedy and adversity in our own lives. Nevertheless, today we find ourselves embroiled in a different kind of war.

Our lives seem to be under constant assault. Worry, fear, stress, and anxiety make war on many of us daily. Our society has accepted depression and discouragement as common social ailments. Anxiety threatens to immobilize us, as unfulfilled dreams, loss, divorce, sickness, death, failures, mistakes, and criticism seem to rain down on us like bombs.

But God is not the author or cause of such destructive atrocities. The Bible clearly states in John 10:10 that Satan is the enemy who comes to steal, and to kill, and to destroy. Jesus came that we might have life—and life more abundantly.

So where do we turn in these trying times? The same place the Christians in World War II did: prayer.

Just as with the British facing the threat of German invasion, we must "Keep Calm and Carry On." When adversity comes, however, simply keeping calm is not enough. We cannot fight the enemy of our soul with a slogan. Nor can we "carry on" in our own strength. We need to rely on and gain our strength from God. We need to trust Him completely and totally.

Whether we realize it or not, many of the battles we face in our lives today are spiritual battles, and we cannot win with just our own willpower. When trouble comes your way or when bad news hits you right between the eyes, be determined to replace fear with confidence in God, to replace worry with faith in Him, and to replace anxiety with His peace. Keep calm, and most of all, trust God.

God has promised to never leave you or forsake you. He wants to be a part of your life. When you need His help, all you have to do is ask. In your hour of greatest need, He will uphold you and sustain you. He will give you peace in the midst of the storms of life.

Our hope is that the following pages will provide encouragement, strength, and inspiration to overcome whatever challenges you may be facing in your life. God is on your side; God is for you! He will see you through!

"There is no medicine like hope,
no incentive so great, and no tonic
so powerful as expectation of
something better tomorrow"

—ORISON MARDEN

Hope

Contrary to what most people believe, hope is not another name for wishful thinking. Hope is a spiritual force defined as confident trust in God, knowing that He will see you through. When trouble comes, it's good to be diligent and seek wise counsel and to do all you know to do, but never put all your hope in a person or this world's system. You can't put your hope in other people, a doctor, an attorney, or in your own ability. You can't put your hope in a company, political party, or the economy. All those things can change in a blink of an eye.

Instead, put your hope in Someone who will never waver or change. The odds may be stacked against you, and failure and defeat may seem imminent, but take heart! Even after you have exhausted all other options, hope is still alive—and His name is Jesus!

There is not a more sure thing in all the universe than putting your confidence and trust in Jesus. Your whole world could come crashing down around you, and He will still be there to sustain you and take care of you.

He'll shelter you in the storms of life—not just to escape them and hide, but to gain strength and renew your hope. He will sustain you in the middle of life's greatest difficulties. He will give you patience to endure, strength to persevere, and courage to overcome whatever challenges you may be facing. He'll make a way when there seems to be no way out. What's impossible with man is possible with Him!

Always put your hope in Jesus!

Prayer

Lord,

I ask You to help me not lose hope. Help me to focus on You and Your Word and not on the challenges or circumstances in my life. I choose to put my confidence in You and not in this world's system or the wisdom of men. I trust You, Lord, to sustain me and lift me up.

I know You love me and You will never abandon me to face my problems alone. You are my refuge and my shelter from the storms of this life. As I study and meditate on the promises in Your Word, I thank You that my heart is encouraged and my soul is refreshed. I find renewed hope and comfort in Your presence.

Scriptures

The Lord taketh pleasure in them that fear him, in those that hope in his mercy.

—PSALM 147:11

Never lag in zeal and in earnest endeavor; be aglow and burning with the Spirit, serving the Lord. Rejoice and exult in hope; be steadfast and patient in suffering and tribulation; be constant in prayer.

—ROMANS 12:11, 12 (AMP)

Wait and hope for and expect the Lord; be brave and of good courage and let your heart be stout and enduring. Yes, wait for and hope for and expect the Lord.

—PSALM 27:14 (AMP)

Who by him do believe in God, that raised him up from the dead, and gave him glory; that your faith and hope might be in God.

—1 PETER 1:21

"A Christian will part with anything rather than his hope; he knows that hope will keep the heart both from aching and breaking, from fainting and sinking; he knows that hope is a beam of God, a spark of glory, and that nothing shall extinguish it till the soul be filled with glory."

—THOMAS BROOKS.

"There is no pit so deep that God's love is not deeper still."

—CORRIE TEN BOOM
(HOLOCAUST SURVIVOR)

Love

Unconditional love—love so pure, so grand, that God would give up His only Son for you. It's a love that says that no matter what you have done, no matter how many mistakes you have made or ever will make, He forgives you and loves you. You might be saying, "How can this be possible? I have messed up so bad, so many times." That's because you don't deserve it, you can't earn it—it is God's *gift* to you. Your actions or goodness are not what qualifies you for the love of God. It is what Jesus did on the cross for you!

God wants us to make prayer and reading His Word a priority in our lives so He can be closer to us. His Word isn't full of rules to restrict us, but rather directions to guide us. He wants us to read His Word because it reveals the splendor of His character. He wants us to pray so He can spend some alone time with us. We don't pray or read the Bible because we *have* to, but because we *want* to be closer to God, who gave everything for us.

God is on your side, He is for you, and He is there to help you. When you miss the mark, the simple truth is God is not disappointed in you, but disappointed *for* you. He isn't mad at you. He just knows when we make bad decisions or let sin into our life that it sets us on a course going the wrong direction. He knows the fear, pain, and heartache waiting at the end of that road. When you mess up or sin, just ask the Lord to forgive you—and then receive that forgiveness. God loves you more than you can ever imagine.

Prayer

Lord,

Thank You for loving me, even when I am unlovely, even when I make mistakes, even when I mess up, and even when I fail You. Help me to trust in Your unconditional love and know that no matter what I do, Your love for me will never change.

Let me grasp the great love that You have for me. Fill my heart with Your love for humanity. Help me express Your love to others. Help me let Your love, Your light, and Your life shine through my life to those around me.

Let Your love be the life force that sustains me in difficult times and guides me when I am unsure what to do. Help me love You with all my heart, soul, and strength and love others like You have loved me. Thank You, Lord, for Your boundless love.

Scriptures

So now faith, hope, and love abide, these three; but the greatest of these is love.

—1 CORINTHIANS 13:13 (ESV)

For God so greatly loved and dearly prized the world that He [even] gave up His only begotten (unique) Son, so that whoever believes in (trusts in, clings to, relies on) Him shall not perish (come to destruction, be lost) but have eternal (everlasting) life.

—JOHN 3:16 (AMP)

We love him, because he first loved us..

—1 JOHN 4:19

By this shall all men know that ye are my disciples, if ye have love one to another.

—JOHN 13:35

It's the definition of God,
The very reason we were spared from his rod.
Instead he gave us his son,
And in death the job was done,

When the pain of living is high,
And it's tough to muster a sigh,
When your heart is vacant of care,
And the weight too much to bare,

When this whole thing we call life feels
like a loss,
It's time you remembered it wasn't nails
that held him to the cross,
It was the greatest strength clothed in
purity like a dove,
The most beautiful and rare element
called Love.

—By Jake Provance

"I love those who can smile in trouble, who can gather strength from distress, and grow brave by reflection."

—LEONARDO DA VINCI

Strength

Sometimes the daily grind of everyday life can rob you of your strength, leaving you tired, beat up, and worn out. Many times it's not just the physical drain but also the mental fatigue that worry, anxiety, and frustration can bring into your life, sapping your strength to the point that you feel completely void of energy.

Maybe things are not going well at work and it takes all the strength you can muster just to get up and go to work every day. Maybe you have lost your job or you are facing the stress of a major sickness in your life or the life of a family member. Maybe you are facing serious marital problems or dealing with a troubled teen. Whatever the case, it takes strength to combat the weariness that comes when trying to balance all the things in our lives. So the question is,

"How can we stay strong in the midst of life's ever-constant troubles?"

God answers this question in His Word and reveals who our source of strength is: "In conclusion, be strong in the Lord [be empowered through your union with Him]; draw your strength from Him [that strength which His boundless might provides]" (Ephesians 6:10 AMP). We gain strength through our fellowship with Him in prayer and through His Word. When we spend time with the Lord, it strengthens our spirit and bolsters our faith. When we read the Bible and meditate on its promises, we receive strength to endure, power to overcome, and joy to sustain us—no matter what challenges may come.

Prayer

Lord,

I ask You to give me strength. Help me draw strength from You so that the demands of daily living won't pull me down or wear me out. Let Your strength produce spiritual resilience, physical stamina, and mental sharpness in me.

Help me resist the temptation to give in or give up. For when my strength begins to waver, Yours will take over. Help me draw strength from You so I will not grow weary. You are my source of energy and my source of strength.

In Your presence I find strength to endure, power to overcome, and sustaining joy to conquer any challenge that may come my way. As I study and meditate on Your Word, I thank You that I find comfort and peace and my strength is renewed.

Scriptures

He giveth power to the faint; and to them that have no might he increaseth strength.

—Isaiah 40:29

But they that wait upon the Lord shall renew their strength; they shall mount up with wings as eagles; they shall run, and not be weary; and they shall walk, and not faint.

—Isaiah 40:31

I have strength for all things in Christ Who empowers me [I am ready for anything and equal to anything through Him Who infuses inner strength into me; I am self-sufficient in Christ's sufficiency].

—Philippians 4:13 (AMP)

"You gain strength, courage and confidence by every experience in which you really stop to look fear in the face. You are able to say to yourself, 'I have lived through this horror. I can take the next thing that comes along.' You must do the thing you think you cannot do."

—ELEANOR ROOSEVELT

"Lord, make me an instrument of your peace. Where there is hatred, let me sow love; where there is injury, pardon; where there is doubt, faith; where there is despair, hope; where there is darkness, light; where there is sadness, joy.

O, Divine Master, grant that I may not so much seek to be consoled as to console; to be understood as to understand; to be loved as to love; For it is in giving that we receive; it is in pardoning that we are pardoned; it is in dying that we are born again to eternal life."

—St Francis of Assisi

Peace

It seems like we are all constantly searching for more peace in our lives. Every day our peace is under constant attack. The flow of text messages and emails from friends, family, and people we don't even know; the daily grind of work and everyday living; and the challenges that life throws at us on a regular basis can stress us out to the point there is no peace in our lives.

But is peace just the lack of feeling stressed, tired, or anxious? Can it be gained by a quiet evening, reading a novel, or watching a favorite show on TV? Maybe temporarily, but that kind of peace is fleeting and dissipates the moment you step back into the real world.

When Jesus left this earth after being resurrected, He said, "Peace I leave with you; my peace I give unto you; not as the world giveth, give I unto you, let not your heart be troubled, neither let it be afraid" John 14:27. Our minds and emotions can't comprehend how we can be calm, cool, and collected in the middle of the craziness of life.

It's not the world's fleeting peace gained from external leisure, but rather an ever-lasting peace that comes from our trust in God. In Isaiah chapter 26, God says, "I will keep them in perfect peace whose eyes are fixed on me." If you need more peace in your life, then maybe you need to change where you are looking! When you choose to look to God and trust Him to take care of you and sustain you, then the busyness of life will cease to overwhelm you and His peace will bring you to a state of calmness and joy that can only come from Him.

Prayer

Lord,

I thank You for giving me Your peace. That peace that passes all understanding. Peace that allows me to face any problem or challenge in my life without getting fretful, disturbed, or anxious. Help me not to be distraught or frustrated when unexpected glitches or difficulties pop up in my life.

Show me how to enter into that place of rest and peace that can only be found in Your presence. Help me to not react badly or become agitated because of what other people say or do. Help me to keep my mind at peace and my heart steady when I am tempted to worry or become fearful because of the circumstances around me. Help me to have confident assurance in the fact that everything will work out just fine if I will keep calm and put my trust in You.

Scriptures

Peace I leave with you, my peace I give unto you: not as the world giveth, give I unto you. Let not your heart be troubled, neither let it be afraid.

—John 14:27

Thou wilt keep him in perfect peace, whose mind is stayed on thee: because he trusteth in thee.

—Isaiah 26:3

And let the peace (soul harmony which comes) from Christ rule (act as umpire continually) in your hearts [deciding and settling with finality all questions that arise in your minds, in that peaceful state] to which as [members of Christ's] one body you were also called [to live]. And be thankful (appreciative), [giving praise to God always].

—Colossians 3:15 (AMP)

And God's peace [shall be yours,
that tranquil state of a soul assured
of its salvation through Christ, and
so fearing nothing from God and
being content with its earthly lot of
whatever sort that is, that peace]
which transcends all understanding
shall garrison *and* mount guard
over your hearts and minds in
Christ Jesus.

—PHILIPPIANS 4:7 (AMP)

"Courage doesn't always roar. Sometimes courage is the little voice at the end of the day that says I'll try again tomorrow."

—MARY ANNE RADMACHER

Courage

When most of us think of courage, we think about acts of heroism on the field of battle, a fireman running into a burning building to rescue a small child from certain death, or a complete stranger diving into a flood-swollen stream to save an elderly woman just before her car is engulfed by the rising waters.

In truth, acts of courage are often more mundane and much less dramatic, but no less significant. An act of courage is when a dad wakes up at 5:00 a.m. every day to go to work at a job he may not enjoy. He may never receive any special recognition or be justly rewarded for his efforts, but he does it anyway to provide for his family. That's courageous.

Sometimes it takes courage to smile when you feel like crying or to be a source of encouragement for others when you are feeling discouraged yourself. It takes courage to let go of the past and forgive, and it takes courage to keep on keeping on when everything inside you says to give up.

So how do you gain courage when you don't think you can bear one more day? Simple—remember what you are fighting for and who you are fighting with. There are things in life worth fighting for, and regardless of what your daily opposition is, it's no match for God! Knowing God is on your team will give you courage to face each day with strength! He's right there with you. He won't let you down and He won't ever leave you. Whatever you're facing, whatever challenge may be looming in your life, this is what God is saying to you: "This is my command—be strong and courageous! Do not be afraid or discouraged. For the Lord your God is with you wherever you go" Joshua 1:9 (NLT).

Prayer

Lord,

Help me to face the uncertainties of this life with an undaunted spirit of courage and confidence. Courage to fight for what I believe in; courage to be unshakeable in my faith; courage to have the determination never to quit or give in when times are tough.

Help me to continually remember that I can do all things through You. Even though I may feel weak or fearful at times, I know You are not. With You on my side I can overcome anything.

I draw my strength from my union with You. Help me have complete confidence in Your ability in me and through me to face any problem or overcome any difficulty. Grant me boldness that I may face any situation with firmness of purpose and a strong resolve. Through You I am more than a conqueror and a world overcomer.

Scriptures

Be strong and of a good courage, fear not, nor be afraid of them: for the Lord thy God, he it is that doth go with thee; he will not fail thee, nor forsake thee.

—DEUTERONOMY 31:6

This is my command—be strong and courageous! Do not be afraid or discouraged. For the Lord your God is with you wherever you go.

—JOSHUA 1:9 (NLT)

Be ye strong therefore, and let not your hands be weak: for your work shall be rewarded.

—2 CHRONICLES 15:7

Be on your guard; stand firm in the faith; be courageous; be strong.

—1 CORINTHIANS 16:13 (NIV)

"Be calm and strong and patient.
Meet failure and disappointment
with courage. Rise superior to the
trials of life and never give in to
hopelessness or despair."

—Dr William Osler

"Great faith is the product of great fights, great testimonies are the outcome of great tests, great triumphs can only come out of great trials, every stumbling block must become a stepping stone and every opposition must become an opportunity."

—Smith Wigglesworth

Faith

What is faith? Simply put, faith is trusting God. It is believing in something you can't see but you know in your heart is true anyway. Faith is the key that opens the door to all of God's blessings. Faith is what activates God to move on your behalf. It is the catalyst that produces an environment for the miraculous to manifest in your life. Faith is essential to receiving anything from God. In fact, the Bible tells us that it's impossible to please God without it.

As you take time to get to know God personally through prayer and His Word, faith will come alive in your heart. When you read and meditate on God's promises, your faith will grow stronger and stronger. When you pray and read His Word, you expand your knowledge of who God is, what He has already done for you, and what He has promised He will do for you. As you get to know God more intimately, it becomes easier to have faith in Him and His willingness to play a major part in your life.

Faith gives us confidence that He will bring to pass whatever He has promised to do. Sometimes faith is just saying, "I trust you Lord," even when you don't know what to do or what to say. It's saying, "Lord, I trust that your love for me is greater than my doubts, my fears, and all my shortcomings," and that somehow He will make a way. It could be even the simplest of all prayers: "Help me, Lord!" knowing that *He will*. Faith is knowing that you are His child and that His desire is to see you happy, blessed, and at peace. It's trusting Him to do what you can't do.

Prayer

Lord,

I ask that You would increase my awareness of You in my everyday life. I know that my faith in You grows as my relationship with You grows. So help me to take time out of my day to pray so I can talk to You, and help me to read Your Word so I can hear what You are saying to me.

I ask that You would help me trust You more fully with all my obligations in life. Help me remember that You are always with me so when things get tough, my faith in You will see me through whatever I face.

Finally, Lord, I sincerely ask for Your patience with me as I learn to trust You wholly in every area of my life. Thank You, Lord, in Jesus' name.

Scriptures

For [if we are] in Christ Jesus, neither circumcision nor uncircumcision counts for anything, but only faith activated and energized and expressed and working through love.

—Galatians 5:6 (AMP)

So then faith cometh by hearing, and hearing by the word of God.

—Romans 10:17

For we walk by faith, not by sight.

—2 Corinthians 5:7

For whatsoever is born of God overcometh the world: and this is the victory that overcometh the world, even our faith.

—1 John 5:4

NOW FAITH is the assurance (the confirmation, the title deed) of the things [we] hope for, being the proof of things [we] do not see and the conviction of their reality [faith perceiving as real fact what is not revealed to the senses].

—HEBREWS 11:1 (AMP)

"How would your life be different
if you learned to let go of things
that have let go of you?
From relationships long gone,
to old grudges, to regrets, to all
the could've' and should've,'....
Free yourself from the burden
of a past you cannot change."

—Dr. Steve Maraboli

Casting Your Cares

These are crazy times. Terrorism is an ever-present danger around the world and even right here at home. The economy is in a constant state of flux and the national debt is out of control. New disease threats like Ebola and superbugs that are resistant to all known antibiotics are popping up at an unprecedented rate. No matter who is in the White House, or what political party has control of Congress, nothing seems to get done. We also find ourselves vulnerable to unconventional enemies like identity theft and cyber-terrorism.

Add to that the personal challenges of everyday life such as job loss, divorce, or health problems, and it can all seem like too much to endure. It is easy to become over-whelmed by a sense of hopelessness. If we are not careful, we can let the cares of this life make us want to crawl into a hole and hide.

But I have some very good news for you. You are not in this battle alone! Jesus told us that in this life we would see and experience some scary stuff, but that we should be of good cheer and not worry because no matter what happens, He will take care of us. He said that the righteous would have many afflictions, but He would deliver us from them all. The Bible also tells us to cast the whole of our care on Him—all our anxieties, all our worries, and all our concerns, because He cares for us and doesn't want us to be burdened with the troubles of this life.

Jesus said, "Come to Me, all you who labor and are heavy-laden *and* overburdened, and I will cause you to rest. [I will ease and relieve and refresh your souls]" Matthew 11:28 (AMP).

Today, give Jesus all your care and rest in Him.

Prayer

Lord,

You said in Your Word that although we would have various problems in this world, that You would deliver us from them all. I ask that You would remind me of this promise daily, so I would not take on all the weight of these problems as burdens in my thought life.

No matter the size, big or small, I know that You want me to be free from all care and worry. Help me grow more reliant on You, so I will not fret over the little stuff that happens in my life. Remind me of the truth of my situation—that no amount of worrying will help me, my friends, or my family. Only You can help.

Lord, I ask that You take these cares that I am carrying, so I may be free to live this life full of joy and peace.

Scriptures

Casting the whole of your care, all your anxieties, all your worries, all your concerns, once and for all on Him, for He cares for you affectionately and cares about you watchfully.

—1 PETER 5:7 (AMP)

Come unto me, all ye that labour and are heavy laden, and I will give you rest.

—MATTHEW 11:28

Cast your cares on the LORD and he will sustain you; he will never let the righteous be shaken.

—PSALMS 55:22 (NIV)

He cares for you,
and knows your troubles too
so cast each one upon Him
and watch what He will do.

He cares for you,
knows each hair on your head
and all of His little sparrows
God has always fed.

He cares for you,
let not anxiety be your guide
humble yourself before Him
and He'll never leave your side.

He cares for you,
are you not just as splendid
as all the lilies in the field
to which He has always tended.

He cares for you,
and carries your burdens too
so, submit your life to Him
and trust in what He can do!

—DEBORAH ANN BELKA

"Bad things do happen: how I respond to them defines my character and the quality of my life. I can choose to sit in perpetual sadness, immobilized by the gravity of my loss, or I can choose to rise from the pain and treasure the most precious gift I have—life itself."

—WALTER ANDERSON

Facing a Crisis

Big or small, it is important to realize that crisis is normal to life. It could be as routine as your child forgetting their lunch or backpack and having to make an unexpected trip to school during a busy day, a flat tire on the highway, or your laptop crashing during a presentation at work. Or it could be something more significant like losing your job, a major illness, a divorce, or the death of a loved one. Large or small, they seem to pop up on a regular basis. There is no such thing as a trouble-free life. When we find ourselves in a crisis, we often keep asking ourselves *why*. But no amount of soul-searching, complaining, or frustration will change our circumstances. In moments of crisis, the best question to ask is, "What do I need to do now?"

The answer is not to fill your mind with questions that have no answer, but rather look to God and His Word. Gather your emotions, keep calm, and trust God. With Him, all things are possible. No crisis is bigger than your God. He is ready and able to move on your behalf and bring deliverance to any situation. As you pray and meditate on His Word, He will provide peace, clarity of thought, and insight concerning your situation. As you look to Him in faith, He will give you guidance, wisdom, and direction on how to navigate your way through whatever crisis you might be facing.

God has promised that He will give us strength and patience to endure and the power to overcome any crisis in our lives. If we put our trust and confidence in Him, then He will always see us through.

Prayer

Lord,

I realize that crisis is a normal part of life. The Bible says that "many are the afflictions of the righteous, but the Lord delivers him out of them all." Thank You, Lord, for Your deliverance.

Help me to be patient and trusting when I face difficulties in my life. Help me to not become fearful, anxious, or overwhelmed when I find myself in a crisis situation. Help me not to react in confusion, worry, or desperation. Show me how to keep a good attitude and a cheerful heart no matter what I am facing. Help me to keep my mind fixed on You—knowing that You will see me through. Give me wisdom and insight concerning any decisions I need to make or actions I need to take.

Thank You for giving me courage, strength, and fortitude to not give up or give in, but to keep trusting You until this crisis is resolved.

Scriptures

Is anyone crying for help? GOD is listening, ready to rescue you.

If your heart is broken, you'll find GOD right there; if you're kicked in the gut, he'll help you catch your breath.

Disciples so often get into trouble; still, GOD is there every time.

—PSALM 34:17-19 (MSG)

..I have learned in any and all circumstances the secret of facing every situation, whether well-fed or going hungry, having a sufficiency *and* enough to spare or going without *and* being in want. I have strength for all things in Christ Who empowers me [I am ready for anything and equal to anything through Him Who infuses inner strength into me; I am self-sufficient in Christ's sufficiency].

—PHILIPPIANS 4:12B-13 (AMP)

When written in Chinese,
the word 'crisis' is composed of
two characters. One represents
danger and the other represents
opportunity.

Danger   Opportunity

"Be of good cheer, do not think of today's failures, but of the success that may come tomorrow. You have set yourselves a difficult task but you will succeed if you persevere; and you will find joy in overcoming obstacles. Remember, no effort that we make to attain something better is ever wasted."

—HELEN KELLER

Press On

There is a lot to be said for persistence. Things often seem to work out for those daring few who refuse to give up—who refuse to quit when things get rough. Whatever you are going through, whatever challenges are in your life, be encouraged. press on! Many times, it's persistence that wins the day.

Sure, the drudgery of life can wear you down. Setbacks, unforeseen delays, or obstacles can cause us to grow weary in the pursuit of goals and dreams, but that is no reason to give up. Too many people quit right before the breakthrough would have come! It's *always* too soon to quit, even if you feel like your back is against the wall and you can't see a way out. That's not the time to whine and complain and get discouraged; it's the time to stand your ground and be determined that you are not going to let the circumstances of life defeat you.

I dare you to refuse to go through life as a victim, but rather a victor. I dare you to press on! You can overcome—not in your own strength, but with God's help. Say to yourself every day, "I can do all things through Christ who strengthens me" and "If God be for me, then no one can be against me." Tell yourself, "I am more than a conqueror through Christ Jesus" and "Thanks be unto God who always causes me to triumph in Christ." As you speak His Word over your life, you will feel His strength rise up in you. He will give you the strength and courage to press on even in the most difficult of situations.

Prayer

Lord,

Please help me to press on and persevere. When it seems everything is stacked against me, remind me that You are always with me. When it feels as though the situations in my life are too much for me to handle, remind me that I'm not handling them alone.

When it's the day-to-day grind that has slowly eroded away my tenacity to keep going, remind me who I'm doing it for. When the bills seem to overwhelm and my energy seems to have all but evaporated, remind me that You are my source and You never run dry.

No matter what this life throws at me, no matter who doubts me, no matter where I find myself, I know that You are my God and You will see me through to the other side!

Scriptures

And let us not grow weary of doing good, for in due season we will reap, if we do not give up.

—GALATIANS 6:9 (ESV)

God is our refuge and strength, a very present help in trouble.

—PSALMS 46:1

But in all these things we overwhelmingly conquer through Him who loved us.

—ROMANS 8:37 (NASB)

I can do all things through Christ which strengtheneth me.

—PHILIPPIANS 4:13

What shall we then say to these things? If God be for us, who can be against us?

—ROMANS 8:31

Henry Ford—failed and went broke five times before he succeeded. Never Quit!

R. H. Macy—failed 7 times before his store in New York City caught on. He Never Quit!

Walt Disney—was fired by a newspaper editor because "he lacked imagination and had no good ideas." He went bankrupt and had several failures before Disney took off.-he didn't quit.

Michael Jordan—was cut from his high school basketball team. He never quit!

Thomas Edison—failed 10,000 times in his attempt to create the light bulb. When questioned later about his failed attempts, he said "I never failed, I just found 10,000 ways it wouldn't work"—he never quit.

Milton Hershey—failed at his first two attempts to start a candy company losing all his money. He didn't quit!

Press on when the going gets tough and let your legacy be like those who never quit.

"We should be too big to take offense and too noble to give it."

—ABRAHAM LINCOLN

Be Not Offended

Offense is a subtle enemy that can creep into your life unnoticed. It can come by way of an inconsiderate driver, a rude co-worker, or an insensitive boss. Maybe a family member or a close friend said something in the heat of the moment that you know they didn't mean, but it still hurt anyway.

We all have plenty of opportunities to get offended on a daily basis and if we aren't careful, it can soon engulf every thought and grow into bitterness. Your first reaction is usually a combination of being hurt and angry. Then you want justice for what was done to you. You may even picture it in your mind, seeing the car that cut you off being pulled over by a police officer or imagining your boss being chewed out by his boss. You may think that if these things were to happen, you would feel better—but the truth is you wouldn't.

It's natural to feel these things, but I encourage you to cut off this way of thinking as soon as you recognize it. The "justice" you seek will not give you the satisfaction you are looking for. Don't let someone else's actions dominate your thoughts and rob you of your joy.

There is a way to guard yourself from being offended. It's to be like God—to forgive and forget when someone sins against you. God wants the best for you, and He knows that when you are dwelling on what has been done to you, you are not thinking about what *He* did for you. When you choose to forgive and not dwell on others' offenses, you will rise above and allow God to keep you in His peace with a smile on your face.

Prayer

Lord,

I ask that You would grant me the ability to see people the way You see them. You love me so unconditionally, regardless of my many offenses against You. Help me to draw on that love so I can show that same love to all those around me.

I ask that You would help me stay calm and in control of my emotions any time an opportunity for offense may come my way. Help me remember to take a breath when people are rude to me, and realize that You are my source. I ask that You remove any bitterness or grudges that I am holding onto in my heart. I know it only hurts me, so please give me the strength to forgive and the peace to forget. Thank You, Lord, for helping me be free to enjoy life.

Scriptures

The one who forgives an offense seeks love, but whoever repeats a matter separates close friends.

—PROVERBS 17:9 (NET)

Understand [this], my beloved brethren. Let every man be quick to hear [a ready listener], slow to speak, slow to take offense and to get angry.

—JAMES 1:19 (AMP)

Above all things have intense and unfailing love for one another, for love covers a multitude of sins [forgives and disregards the offenses of others].

—1 PETER 4:8 (AMP)

Good sense makes one slow to anger, and it is his glory to overlook an offense.

—PROVERBS 19:11 (ESV)

And blessed is the one who is not offended by me.

—LUKE 7:23 (ESV)

"As I walked out the door toward the
gate that would lead to my freedom
I knew if I didn't leave my bitterness
and hatred behind I would still be
in prison."

—NELSON MANDELA
(AFTER 27 YEARS OF WRONGFUL IMPRISONMENT)

To forgive is to set a prisoner free
and discover the prisoner was you.

—Lewis B. Smedes

Forgiveness

Forgiveness is the cornerstone of the Christian experience. Jesus offers unequivocal forgiveness to everyone who believes in Him and receives Him as Lord. No matter what you have done, no matter how disgraceful your deeds or actions, Jesus is reaching out to you right now and is saying, "I forgive you and I love you." It's the first and greatest miracle of Christianity. Our finite mind can hardly grasp the wonder, scope, and beauty of the Lord's forgiveness. You can't earn it; you don't deserve it. It's God's gift to you.

Now it's your turn. The Bible says we should forgive others just like Christ has forgiven us. Maybe you are harboring unforgiveness in your heart towards someone. It may be because of the betrayal of a close friend, a failed marriage, or a boss that passed you over for a well-deserved promotion. Maybe it's the result of a more serious violation like physical, verbal, or sexual abuse by a close family member when you were a child; or maybe you were the victim of a serious crime. Whatever the case, with God's help you can pass on the gift of forgiveness and experience the freedom that comes through truly forgiving those who have hurt you. God can and will erase the pain, despair, and hatred that has infiltrated your life because of someone else's actions.

And now the toughest of all—you need to forgive *yourself*. Maybe it's your own actions that eat away at you daily, keeping you trapped in a prison of regret. God forgives you, and now you need to forgive yourself and move into the bright and wonderful future that God has destined for you. God wants you to experience the beauty of forgiveness in every area of your life.

True joy brings with it things like enthusiasm for life, determination to hang in there, and a desire to encourage others.

—CHUCK SWINDOL

NOW AVAILABLE

KEEP
CALM
AND
TRUST
GOD

JAKE PROVANCE & KEITH PROVANCE

TOPICS INCLUDE . . . ANXIETY, WORRY, FEAR,
DEPRESSION, PRESSURE , REGRET, STRESS, FRUSTRATION,
SELF-CRITICISM, AND UNEXPECTED SETBACKS

Prayer

Lord,

Thank You for the awesome gift of Your forgiveness and unconditional love. Since I have been forgiven of so much, help me to be quick to forgive others. I pray for those who have hurt me in any way. I forgive them for anything they have done. I will not hate them, despise them, or desire that they suffer retribution for their actions against me.

I ask You to forgive them as well. I pray that You reach out to them and minister Your loving kindness to them. I release them. I will not gossip, ridicule, or slander their character with others.

Lord, help me to forgive myself for my failures, mistakes, and shortcomings. Help me to receive Your forgiveness so I can put the past behind me and go forward without guilt and condemnation and fulfill the destiny You have for me.

Scriptures

Even if we feel guilty, God is greater than our feelings, and he knows everything. Dear friends, if we don't feel guilty, we can come to God with bold confidence.

—1 JOHN 3:20-21 (NLT)

He canceled the record of the charges against us and took it away by nailing it to the cross.

—COLOSSIANS 2:14 (NLT)

And be ye kind one to another, tenderhearted, forgiving one another, even as God for Christ's sake hath forgiven you.

—EPHESIANS 4:32

"O Lord, remember not only the men and women of good will, but also those of ill will. But do not remember all of the suffering they have inflicted upon us, instead remember the fruits we have borne because of this suffering—our fellowship, our loyalty to one another, our humility, our courage, our generosity, the greatness of heart that has grown from this trouble. When our persecutors come to be judged by you, let all of these fruits that we have borne be their forgiveness."

—(FOUND IN THE CLOTHING OF A DEAD CHILD AT RAVENSBRUCK CONCENTRATION CAMP.)

"Joy is the infallible sign of the presence of God."

—Pierre Teilhard de Chardin

Joy

We all like to be around a joyful or happy person. Often we use the words "joy" and "happiness" interchangeably, but really there is a significant difference. Happiness is a product of our surroundings, but joy, on the other hand, comes from within.

Happiness is a result of what happens *to us*. Joy is a result of what happens *in us*. True joy is an inner strength that comes from our fellowship with Father God. God tells us in His Word that when we are in His company there is fullness of joy and that His joy is a source of strength to us. This joy does not waver in the face of adversity. His joy is a stabilizing force that will sustain us in the storms of life. His joy will give you strength and courage to face any situation with a smile on your face and a song in your heart.

God tells us in His Word to be joyful when we face the trials of this life, knowing that He will take care of us. We're to rejoice and be glad every day, knowing that each day is a gift from Him. If we will make it a priority to live lives of thanksgiving and praise, His joy will fill our hearts. As you spend time with the Lord and put your complete trust and confidence in His love for you, His joy will become grafted into your life. His joy will become your joy. Then, when trouble comes or difficult circumstances pop up, you can face them with an unshakeable joy that will undergird you and sustain you. Make a decision today to let the joy of the Lord rule in your heart!

Prayer

Lord,

Because You love me, You want me to be blessed and fulfilled in every area of my life. I know that true joy comes from You and that You can help me to rejoice even in the midst of disappointments and trials. Let me keep my mind focused on You and what You have done for me and not on the shortcomings of my life or the problems I face.

The Bible says, "This is the day the Lord has made; we will rejoice and be glad in it." I can rejoice because I know that with You I am not alone—You will never leave me or turn away from me.

I ask You to fill my life with Your joy today and every day.

Scriptures

"Strengthened with all might, according to his glorious power, unto all patience and longsuffering with joyfulness;

—COLOSSIANS 1:11

Now the God of hope fill you with all joy and peace in believing, that ye may abound in hope, through the power of the Holy Ghost.

—ROMANS 15:13

"……And be not grieved *and* depressed, for the joy of the Lord is your strength *and* stronghold."

—NEHEMIAH 8:10B (AMP)

My brothers and sisters, think of the various tests you encounter as occasions for joy. After all, you know that the testing of your faith produces endurance.

—JAMES 1:2-3 (CEB)